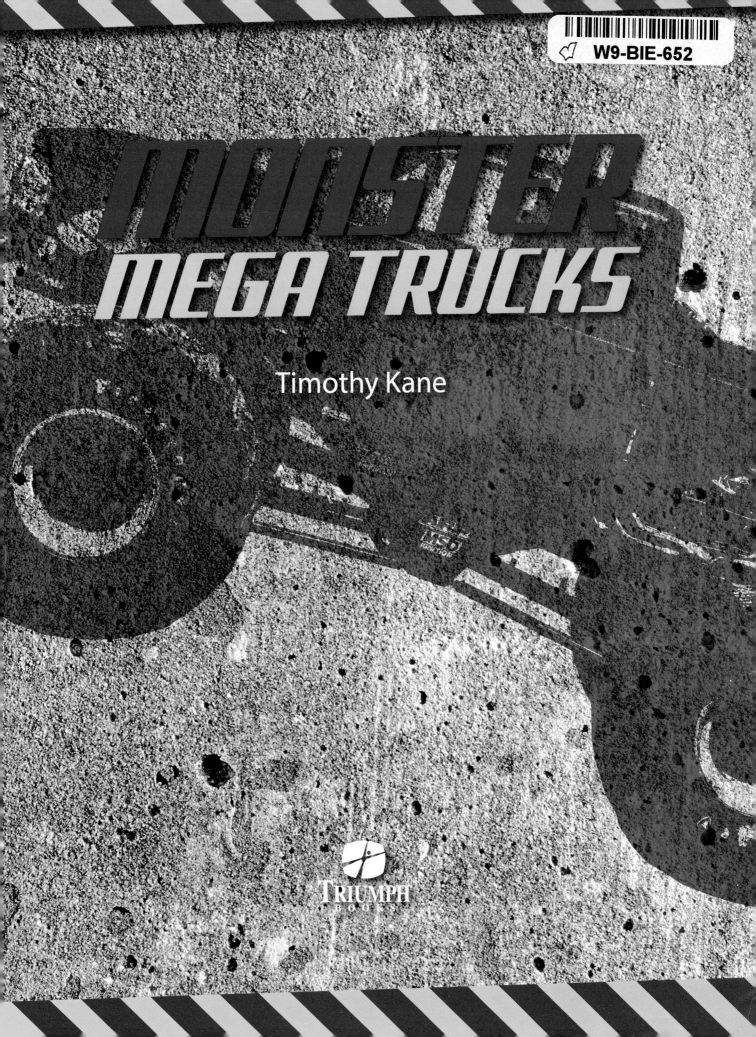

# MONSTER
## MEGA TRUCKS

Timothy Kane

TRIUMPH
BOOKS

This book is available in quantity at special discounts for your group or
organization. For further information, contact:

Triumph Books LLC
814 N. Franklin
Chicago, Illinois 60610
www.triumphbooks.com
Printed in U.S.A.

ISBN: 978-1-62937-035-4

Content developed and packaged by Rockett Media, Inc.
Writer: Timothy Kane
Editor: Bob Baker
Design and page production: Andrew Burwell
All photos courtesy of AP Photos unless otherwise noted.

# MONSTER
## MEGA TRUCKS

# CHAPTER ONE: THE AERODYNAMICS OF BIGFOOT 18

**M**onsters can fly. If you've ever been to a Monster Truck show, then you've seen them soaring through the air. This is not easy when you weigh six tons and have no wings. One of the most famous Monster Trucks, BigFoot, recently made history when it used its newly-found power to take to the skies and break a world record.

If you look on YouTube, you can see the video when Bigfoot broke the Guinness World Record for longest ramp jump by a Monster Truck. Driven by Dan Runte, this oversized vehicle jumped 219 feet, beating the old record of 208 feet. This is the length of about two-thirds of a football field. Imagine the power it took

to make such a leap! Designed especially for the jump, this monster truck – dubbed Bigfoot 18 – weighs six tons, which is about 1,500 pounds heavier than the previous Bigfoot. Along with its new-found weight, it also has a longer chassis, tougher shocks and a sturdier frame. These technological improvements were made with the aim to give Bigfoot 18 more power and better performance.

This new and improved version of Big-foot had to be made sturdier so it could survive the world-record jump. Driver Dan said he had to keep the truck square and straight when it hit the ramp. While airborne, he had to keep his foot on the gas to keep all four wheels spinning so he could land at about 70 miles per hour.

"It's an adrenalin rush every time you get into (a monster truck)," Runte told *Popular Mechanics*.

A newly improved V-8 engine – fueled

## THE 10 SCARIEST MONSTER TRUCKS

1) **Bigfoot**
2) **Snake Bite**
3) **Grave Digger**
4) **Batman**
5) **Jurassic Attack**

6) **El Toro Loco**
7) **Dragon's Breath**
8) **Backwards Bob**
9) **Predator**
10) **Mohawk Warrior**

**Source:** *Motor Trend Magazine*

by alcohol – was developed especially for this world-class feat. It was built closer to the roll cage than the earlier Bigfoot models. The reason for moving the engine forward is to keep the nose of the truck down after it's airborne, which gives it improved aerodynamics and more velocity. The Bigfoot 18 has a 1,550 horse-power engine. This means that it would take 1,550 horses to produce the same amount of power as this engine. It also produces about 1,250 foot-pounds of torque, which is an incredible amount of force. Consequently, the Bigfoot 18's engine lasts only about a year before it conks out due to extreme wear and tear.

The Bigfoot 18 also has a supercharger that increases the truck's power by forcing pressurized air into the engine, allowing for more fuel to burn. Monsters already burn twice as much fuel as ordinary cars, and the Bigfoot 18, with its super strength, drinks even more. A quick-engine shutoff switch has to be used to conserve fuel when Monsters sit idle, so they can retain their power.

The Bigfoot 18 was rebuilt in six months by Bigfoot 4x4, Inc. in Hazelwood, MO.

## CHAPTER TWO:
## MONSTER TRUCKS –
## WEIRD AND WACKY

Decades before the advent of Monster Trucks, kids on road trips, sitting in the back of the family station wagon and tooling down the interstate, used to invent games to pass the time when they were bored. One game was to count the weirdest-looking vehicles they would see on the road.

For example, nothing was better then to see a Volkswagen Beetle – a "slug bug" – and pop your sibling on the shoulder. These cars have a domed-

look that resembles a motorized snow globe. They are funny-looking and you can't help but smile when you see them. Another popular standout is the Smart Car, so named for its excellent gas mileage. However, they look so ridiculously small and boxy, you can't help but think of them as a little toy car. Years ago, there was a car called the AMC Gremlin, named after a fictitious gnome that – as legend has it – was responsible for sabotaging aircraft. The AMC Gremlin was named by *Time* magazine as being among the 50 worst cars of all time and it was quite the sight to see one driving past you. Its odd shape and weird name are reasons why we still recall it today.

As you can see, the ordinary family car is not what gets remembered. Your average four-door sedan is not what people

talk about and is barely noticed. What we like to see and what gets a reaction are things that look novel, unique and different. We want to see vehicles that are so crazy-looking that they are burned into our memory.

People like to see weird, crazy mutants on wheels. And people love to see them in action. If you put them under one roof and invite the public, you have a Monster Truck rally, with giant beastly trucks racing, doing donuts, making leaps and driving over the top of junk-yard relics.

Such interest in the unusual and being different is the reason why there are Monster Trucks in the first place. Bob Chandler, called the father of Monster Trucks, is said to be the first known person to put oversized tires on a pickup just so he could smash other cars flat. Chandler was a truck mechanic and decided that he "wanted to be bigger" than everybody else on the road. He put big tires on his pickup so others would notice him (and kids would wave at him

## DUPLICATE DIGGERS

There are nine Grave Diggers being driven by different drivers. Grave Digger is considered to be one of the most influential and iconic Monster Trucks of all time.

as they passed in their station wagons).

Chandler started to run over cars for fun with his giant truck on his Missouri farm in 1981. A show promoter saw a video of his first car crunch and asked him to do it in front of a paying audience. Chandler said he had no idea how popular Monster Trucks would become. He said he originally thought about driving over cars, and he never even considered the boats, buses, trucks or airplanes that Monster Trucks climb and stomp on today. He also said he never imagined the awesome power and force these trucks would generate in order to do their amazing, high-flying stunts.

Decades have passed since that first Monster Truck, the modified pick-up on a farm in Missouri. Today's Monster Trucks continue to mutate, and grow

bigger and stranger. For example, consider the Jurassic Attack, it has three horns and scales like the Triceratops dinosaur, or how about the Grave Digger, that is designed to look like a supercharged funeral hearse. Weird, huh?

## CHAPTER THREE: WHAT'S iT LiKE DRIVING A MONSTER TRUCK?

Talk about multi-tasking, driving a Monster Truck requires that the driver turn the front and the rear wheels at the same time. It can be pretty confusing. Darren Migues, driver of the Red Barron, said that because of its size and the way a Monster Truck is built, two steering mechanisms are a must. It means you have to think about going in two different directions at the same time.

The inside of the Red Barron looks like a space capsule, with exposed wires and gauges. These alert the driver to how his truck is performing. The driver's seat, inside a roll-cage, is super sturdy and welded to the vehicle's frame. The driver is harnessed with multiple seatbelt straps. There is extra protection around the driver's head and neck,

## CAR CRUSH

In just the Monster Jam circuit of truck shows staged around the globe, more than 3,000 cars are crushed every year.

20 14

:55   TIME OUTS LEFT  3

OAKTRONICS

TO GO   BALL ON   QTR.

1

BUD LIGHT

SMOOTH & REFRESHING
12 FL. OZ. • BEER
A B ST. LOUIS, MO

TIME OF DAY

FLORIDA HOSPITAL

FL

MONSTER JAM

## WHEELS OF FORTUNE

A "slap wheelie" is when a Monster Truck's front wheels bounce off the ground and the driver presses down the gas pedal – using the torque of the engine – to push up the front end of the truck into a wheel stand (like a hand stand).  Some drivers famous for performing slap wheelies are Dan Runte (Bigfoot), Paul Shafer (Monster Patrol), Kelvin Ramer (Time Flys) and George Balhan (Mohawk Warrior).

designed to absorb the jerks and jolts when the truck is airborne.

Migues plays down the difficulty of driving his monster, but Peter Cheney, national driving columnist for the Canadian newspaper *Globe and Mail*, gave a spine-chilling account of his first experience behind the wheel of a Monster Truck called Black Stallion.

"Monster trucks don't have doors," he said. "To get up to the cockpit, you climb up through the truck's steel frame, like a roughneck scaling an oilrig. The gas pedal has a hook that goes over your toes, so you can pull it back if the throttle jams – if not, the truck has enough power to launch itself four stories into the air."

## CHAPTER FOUR: THE WOMAN BEHIND SAMSON'S WHEEL

Just a handful of professional Monster Truck drivers are women. One of the few is Allison

Patrick, who shares the same last name with another pioneering female driver -- Danica Patrick of race car driving fame. Allison told the Charleston, W. Va. *Gazette-Mail*, that fans should expect the Old Boy's Club in Monster Trucks to change soon.

"… More and more women are getting involved," Allison said. She is the driver of the popular 10,000 pound, 1,500 horse-power Monster Truck named Samson. The name Samson is ironic, as it is shared with the strong man in the Bible who is defeated by a woman who discovers the secret to his strength. Now Allison is rediscovering the strength of Samson, but her plan is to use it to conquer the Monster Truck world.

Allison, 28, is the daughter of Dan Patrick, a member of the Monster Truck Hall of Fame, and Samson's former driver. He drove Samson for more than 25 years before he turned over the wheel to his daughter. Dan Patrick is now semi-retired, but travels with Allison when she's competing on the road. He works as a member of her pit crew.

"I grew up in it," Allison said and, when her father gave her the opportunity to take over Samson's driving privileges, she quickly accepted. "My dad has had a truck since I was

www.markbrown-studio.com

REG. U.S. PAT ®

FK ROD ENDS

Airgas

Photo Courtesy of Feld Motor Sports

## WHEELY TiRED

Manufactured by Goodyear and Firestone, Monster Truck tires must be at least 66 inches high and 43 inches wide. The average Monster Truck team will go through eight tires in one year. Tires are customized and hand cut to accommodate track conditions. Cutting one tire takes approximately 50 hours. The average cost is $2,600 per tire.

three years old, and I don't see my life as any different."

Allison said she grew up with Monster Trucks and fits right in. According to the Samson website, Allison also has a fulltime job working as nurse in the intensive care unit of Berger Hospital in Circleville, Ohio during the week, so she can continue to drive on the weekends.

# CHAPTER FIVE: MONSTER TRUCKS NOT IMMUNE TO ZOMBIE APOCALYPSE

The only thing that will scare the menacing Monster Trucks Grave Digger and Undertaker is a more frightening monster, especially one that won't stay in the ground – a zombie. This monster is new to the

Monster Truck show scene, and is followed by legions of human zombie fans. If you look closely at the audience, you can find members of the roving undead waiting for their favorite team member, the Zombie Monster Truck. One look at Zombie is enough to give you the shivering creeps.

Even Sean Duhon – Zombie's driver – dresses for the part. He wears ghoulish makeup and spooky-yellow contact lenses. Duhon gives chilling interviews and talks about spreading the Zombie rage like a sickness throughout Mon-

ster Truck fandom. The more he speaks, the more the zombie fan base responds in dress and attitude.

The Zombie is creepy itself with flared nostrils and dead yellow eyes. Plus, the grill of the Zombie is decorated with crooked yellow teeth. There are also bits of fabric – some say tattered, moldy flesh – attached to its blotchy outer shell.

Down in New Orleans, many fans go to shows dressed like zombies and cheer for their favorite monster. Zombie responds by crushing car hulks and driving in crazy donuts, just like a member of the walking dead.

## CHAPTER SIX: TRANSFORMERS

If legend has it - legend according to the Monster Jam website – there is a remote island somewhere in the Pacific Ocean that has become a breeding ground for a number of mutating species. These are supposedly giant beasts not seen on earth since the Jurassic period. These man-eating Monster vehicles had become a threat to the peace-loving inhabitants of the island.

According to the story, the island leadership found a kind of sunken treasure – a

## NEED FOR SPEED:

The top speed for a monster truck is about 70 miles per hour. This is the same as the cheetah, the fastest animal on land.

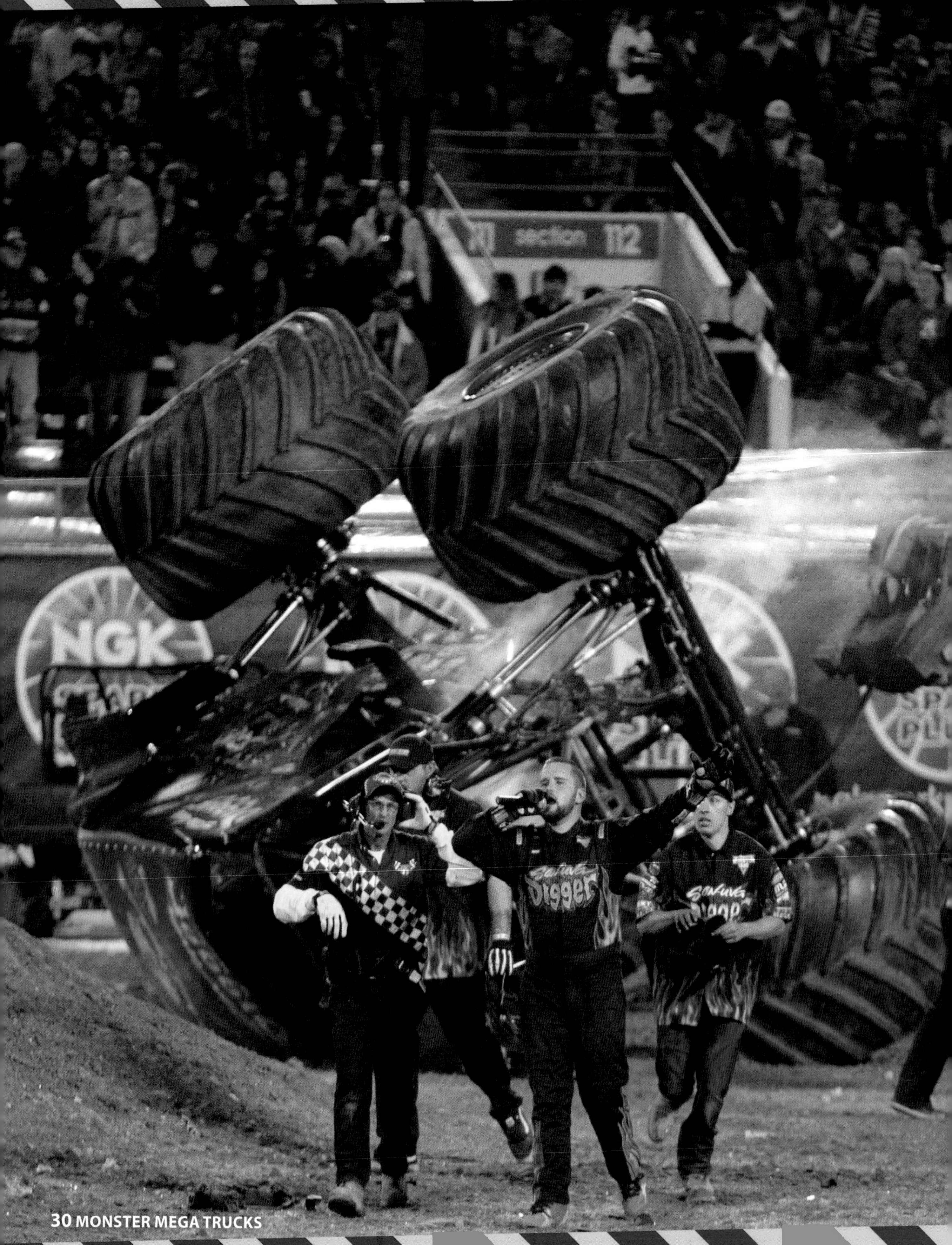
section
112
NGK
Digger

military transport that had foundered offshore in shallow water. In its hold, there were tanks and other armored vehicles. Scientists and engineers on the island were able to use the parts and piece together two mechanical giants – Megasaurus and Transaurus, which are also known as Transformers.

Transformers start off as all-terrain vehicles. They can travel anywhere incognito, transform and then attack. The two mechanical beasts stand three stories tall and weigh about 50,000 pounds. Once built, these Transformers were able to destroy the mutants on the island.

Once captured and taken on tour with the Monster Jam circuit, the Megasaurus and Transaurus now satisfy their appetites by devouring junk cars and soaking up the awe and admiration from appreciative Monster Truck audiences around the world.

# CHAPTER SEVEN:
# A WHALE OF A TRUCK

Let's talk big! Really big!

Caterpillar makes the biggest dump truck of all time, and this giant is a true working monster. It doesn't perform in shows, but has a job instead. The Caterpillar 797 weighs more than 1 million pounds, carries 400 tons and costs $6 million. It's more than 50 feet high - which is five stories tall - and nearly 50 feet long. The 797 would take up three lanes on a highway.

But it's likely you won't see it on the road. Or on stage for that matter.

You'll find the Caterpillar 797 spending its time in big holes in the ground. It was built to handle the toughest jobs for large-scale mining operations. It saves the mining companies money by carrying the heaviest loads.

The design and development of the 797 took years. It was introduced in 1998 and tested at Caterpillar's Arizona proving grounds and at the Bingham Canyon Mine in Utah.

Each wheel is attached to the axle using 47 nuts. The tires are 13 feet tall and weigh

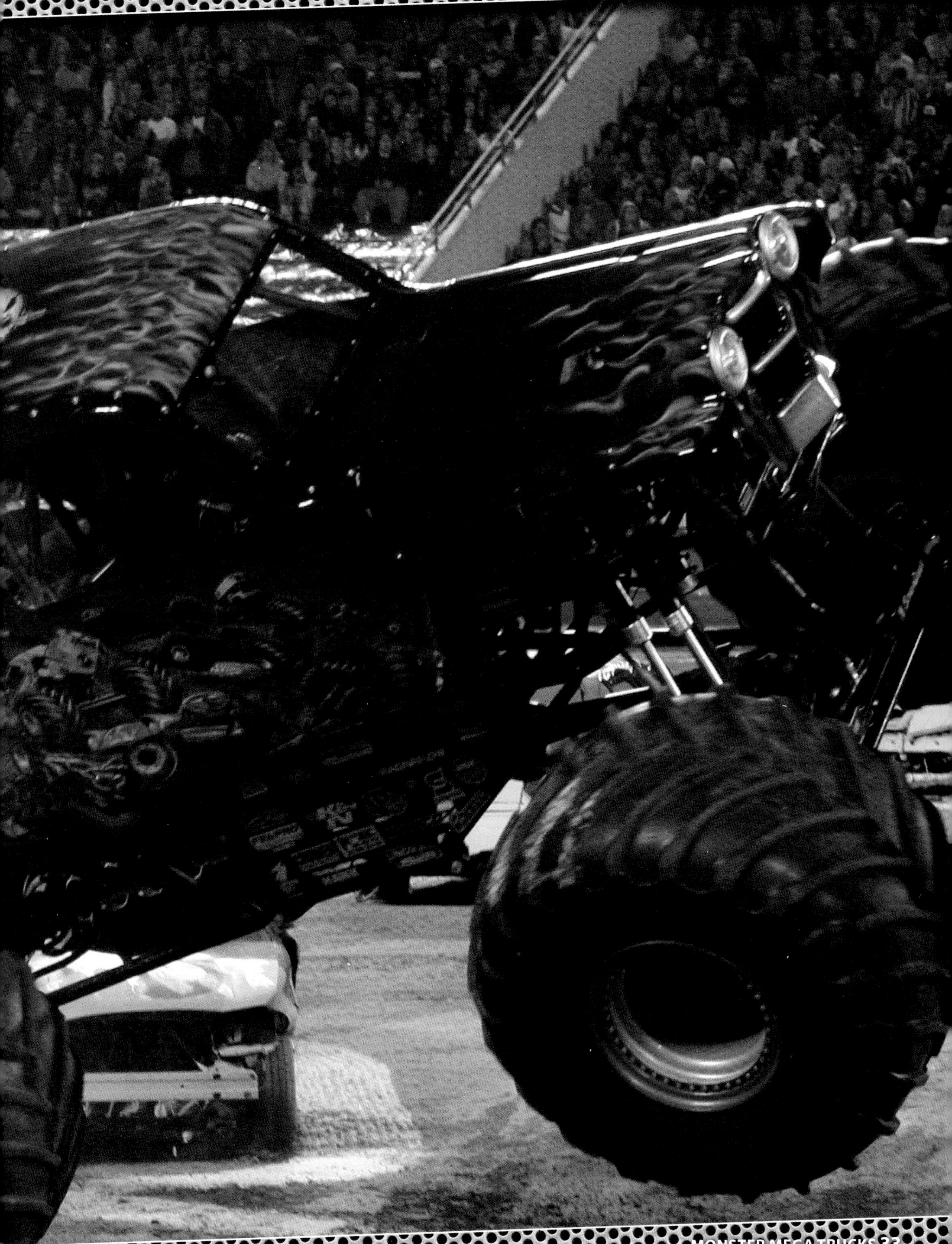

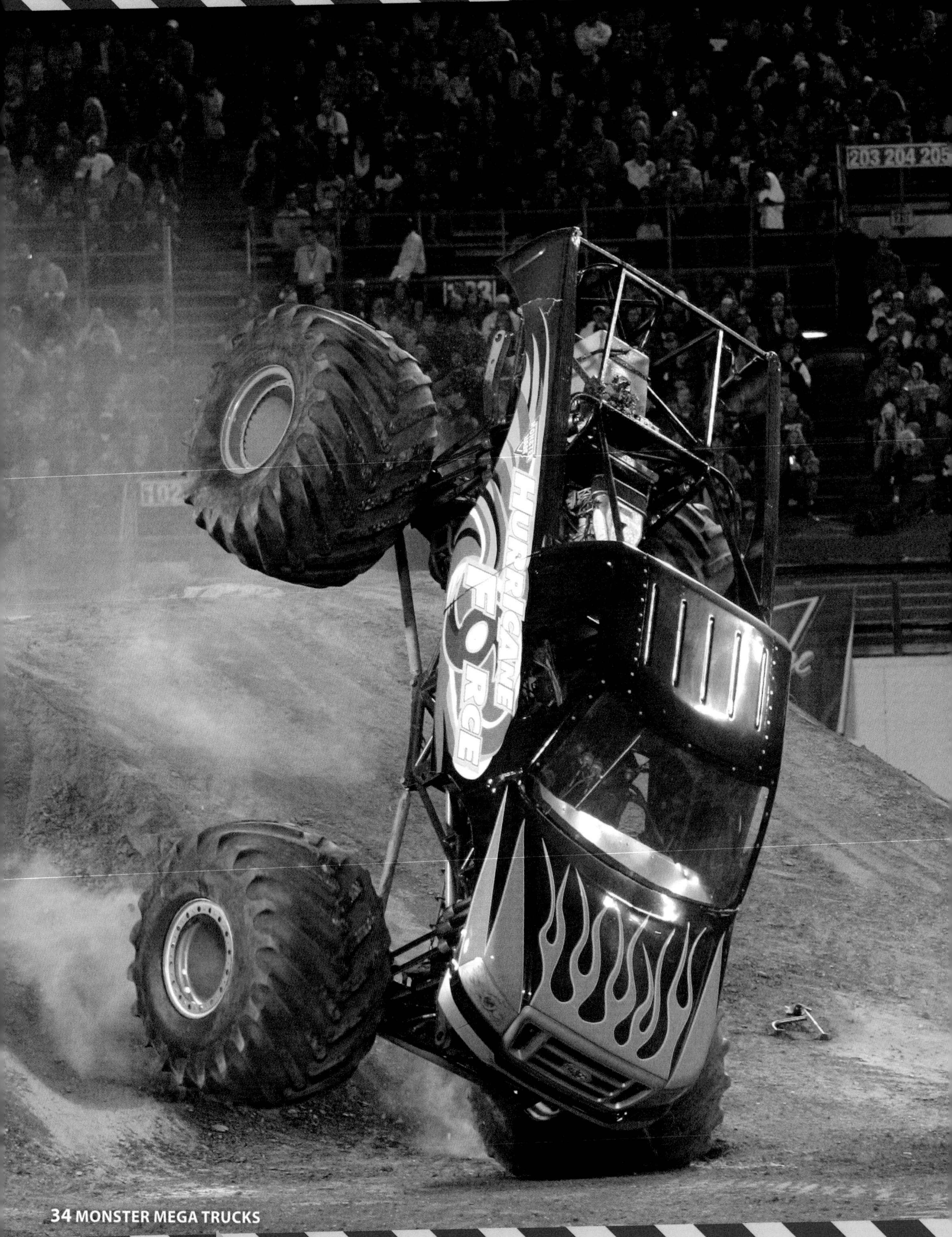
203 204 205
HURRICANE

nearly 12,000 pounds.

"The Caterpillar 797 is the largest truck ever," wrote John Pearley Huffman, for *Car and Driver* magazine. "But unless you work in a mine, you're probably never going to see one. That's a shame, because this is the real thing: a vehicle that's authentically awesome."

The Caterpillar 797 is so big that you cannot tell how big it is by looking at photos of it. You need something in the picture to give it scale, so you can appreciate its massive size.

How big is big? Two semi flatbeds driving next to each other would be needed to transport it on the highway. *Piston Heads* – an online magazine – calls it "Mr. Big Stuff" and describes the Caterpillar 797 like this:

"Frankly, stuff doesn't get much bigger. This behemoth of a vehicle is hard to describe; nothing you'll see in the streets of the world will compare. In fact, you'll never see it on the streets; it's just too big. Its working domain is in the mining environments of the world and that's where it belongs …"

And talk about a gas-guzzler, the Caterpillar 797 goes through 1 gallon a minute. It's tank holds 12,000 gallons. The typical tanker truck that brings the gasoline to the service stations only carries about 5,500 to 11,600 gallons of gasoline.

To be sure, the Caterpillar 797 is a thirsty whale.

## CHAPTER EIGHT: THE YOUNGEST MONSTER TRUCK DRIVER

She's been called the world's youngest Monster Truck driver. Rosalee Ramer – from Watsonville, CA – crushed her first car when she was just 13 years old. She was driving her dad's Monster Truck.

Three years later she appeared on *Ellen*, a daytime talk show, and chatted with the show's host, Ellen DeGeneres.

"The tires are as tall as I am, but they weigh 800 pounds," Rosalee told DeGeneres. DeGeneres seemed genuinely awed when Rosalee demonstrated her driving prowess, running

GRAVE DIGGER

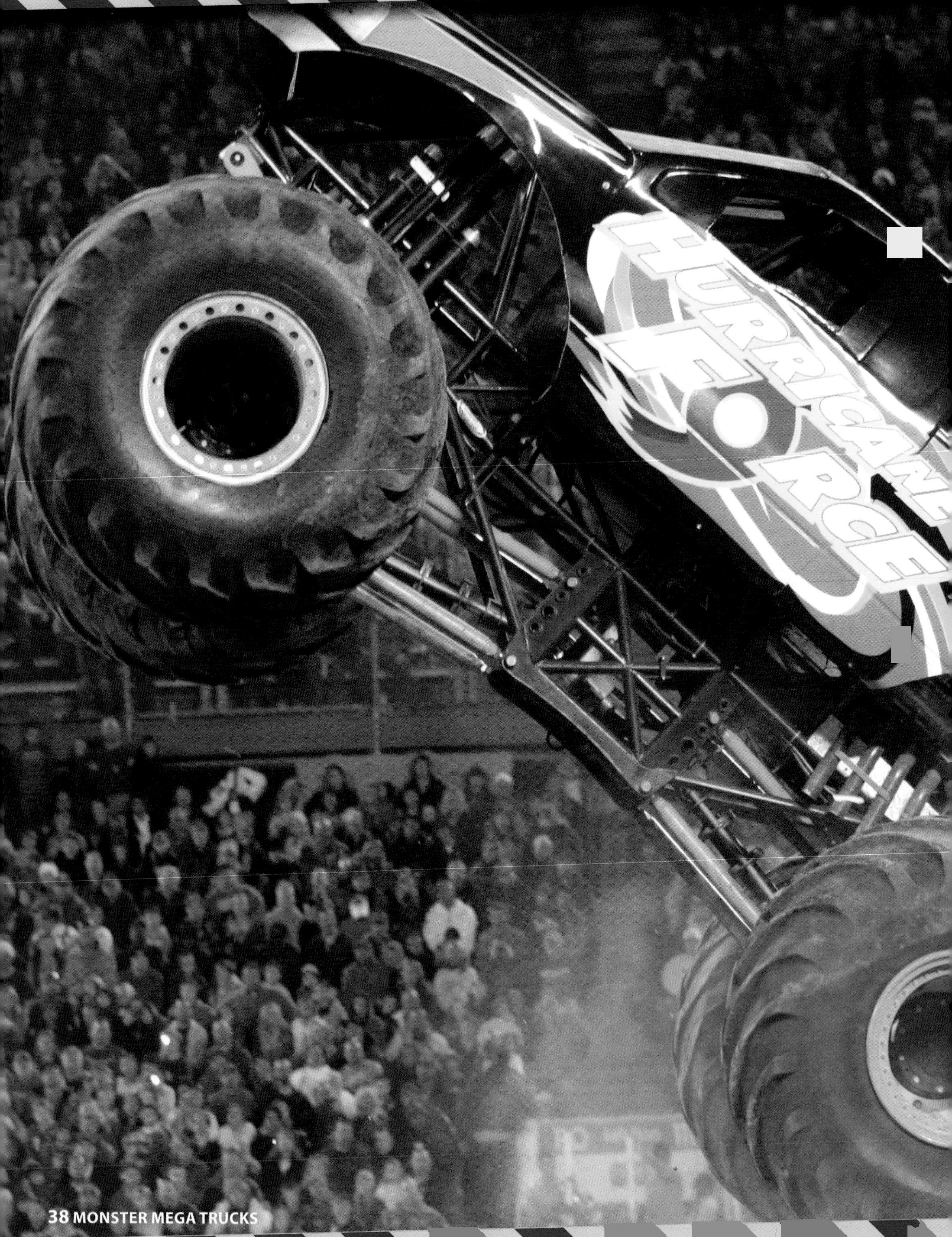
HURRICANE
FORCE

over cars and doing donuts in the studio parking lot.

"Wow!" DeGeneres said. "You kind of think you know what you're going to see. You really can't imagine the excitement when you see something like that! … That was amazing. That was so impressive! I can't get over the fact that you're 16 years old and doing this!"

According to the *San Francisco Chronicle*, Rosalee is a whiz at math and plans to attend an Ivy League school and study engineering.  Kelvin Ramer,

Rosalee's father, told the *Chronicle* that his daughter started getting into Monster Trucks just after she started walking. He remembers Rosalee holding a flashlight when she was a three-year-old, helping he and his buddies work on engines at night.

A Ford Taurus hubcap hangs on the wall of Rosalee's bedroom. "A Monster Truck driver always remembers the first car she smashes," Rosalee said.

Rosalee's Monster Truck driving is getting attention around the world. An article in the *London Daily Mail* reported, "While 16-year-old Rosalee Ramer's peers are just getting used to parallel parking and driving on the freeway, she's behind the wheels of a 10-ton truck, going over 30-foot jumps, crushing smaller cars and popping wheelies as the nation's youngest professional Monster Truck driver."

"Being in a truck with 1,600 horsepower is unlike anything else and stepping on the throttle is amazing", Rosalee told *ABC News*. "It's something that I've dreamt about. And I'm finally doing it. Going over jumps sometimes 25 or 30 feet in the air, I feel like I'm flying."

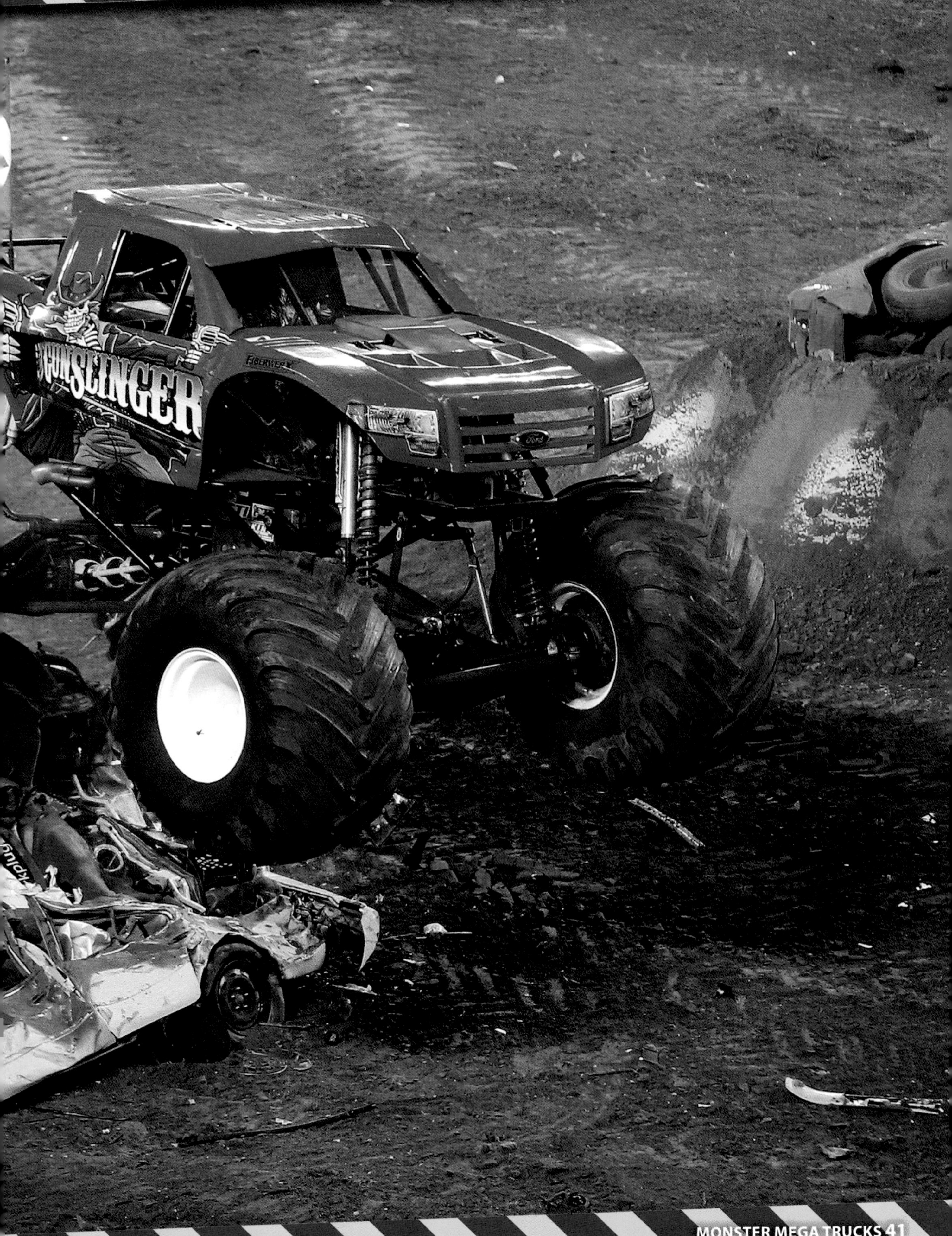
GUNSLINGER

BAD NEWS TRAVELS FAST

Vehicle Wrap By:
SIGN PRO
Harrisonburg, VA
(540) 574-3052
www.MySign9ro.net

YOU LOSE TO BAD NEWS

# CHAPTER NINE: OLD SCHOOL MAKE-YOUR-OWN MONSTER

**M**onster trucks do roam the streets. You may not have seen them. These are the *Street Monsters*, built by loyal fans. They are there, roaming the streets at night, but they didn't come out of the factory that way. These Monsters are like Frankenstein and rebuilt from spare parts.

If you're good with a wrench, you may choose to play the role of the Mad Doctor and do the job yourself. All you need to do is roll up your sleeves and get to work converting your pickup into a Street Monster. There are a number of under-carriage conversion kits available for purchase. Don't forget to add big wheels and a roll bar to give your truck full Monster style.

TED SMAK AT WORK IN HIS MONSTER TRUCK SHOP

Or, if you don't feel comfortable building your own Monster, you can find a good mechanic to do the job. Someone like Ted Smak, who is the owner of a shop called McHenry County 4-Wheel Drive. Smak has been making street Monsters for almost 30 years.

He is his own Dr. Frankenstein, making two to three Monsters every month. They usually start out as Chevy and Ford pickups or, occasionally, a four-door Jeep. The cost of converting a pickup into a Street Monster is $5,000 to $7,000.

"There is a limit to the size of tires you can put on a Street Monster," Smak said. "I replace shocks, stabilizers, and suspension and transfer cases. The trailing arm is replaced with a long arm. And I stabilize the steering."

The main reason to create a Street Monster is to add on bigger tires. Why do these drivers want big tires on their pickups? These Monsters like to explore the fields and the woods.

"You can take your converted pickup for some off-road driving," Smak said. "Big tires make it easier to get through deep mud."

They also like to brag. They get to tell their friends and neighbors that they own the

only Monster on the block.

"People really want a Monster Truck because it's like owning a Porsche or a Corvette. You get noticed. If you're a Monster Truck driver, you stand out in a crowd. People stare at you when you drive by," said Smak.

"The bigger tires on a jacked-up frame also make it easier to find your vehicle in a parking lot. It's taller than the oth-ers. You'll see the top sticking up above the sea of cars."

The important thing is it's your Mon-ster. It is built the way you want it. You have your own Monster and no one else has one.

"It's also a fashion statement. There's not another like it. It's built to your specs. It's one of a kind."

However, owning a Street Monster is

not all fun. There are some drawbacks.

"The biggest problems are it won't fit in an automatic car wash and you won't be able to use parking garages anymore," Smak said. "The ceilings are too low."

How can you spot a Street Monster?

Not only by its size, but after a monster conversion, it's easy to tell the work that was done on a vehicle. The Monster parts are all shiny and new.